**The
Machine
Never Blinks**

Fantagraphics Books, Inc.
7563 Lake City Way NE
Seattle WA 98115
(800) 657-1100
FANTAGRAPHICS.COM

Publisher: GARY GROTH
Senior Editor: J. MICHAEL CATRON
Designers: KEELI McCARTHY and CHELSEA WIRTZ
Production: CHRISTINA HWANG and PAUL BARESH
Associate Publisher: ERIC REYNOLDS

First Fantagraphics Books edition: June 2020
ISBN 978-1-68396-282-3
Library of Congress Control Number: 2019944632
Printed in Singapore

The MACHINE NEVER BLINKS

A GRAPHIC HISTORY OF SPYING AND SURVEILLANCE

By Ivan Greenberg
Illustrated by Everett Patterson
and Joseph Canlas
Foreword by Ralph Nader

Foreword by Ralph Nader

In the 1970s, debates about "invasions of privacy" — a phrase far too benign — centered around wiretapping, credit card information, and the looming "electronic funds transfer." Then, many people shrugged and said, "I've got nothing to hide."

There are far fewer shruggers today. We have since learned that everybody actually does have something to hide — intimate conversations with family, physicians, clergy, attorneys, and accountants, to name just an endangered few. More fundamentally, people today realize that, throughout history, when the powerful want to control the powerless, they do it by ripping privacy aside and using the details of people's personal lives against them. After all, the masses can't all be put into prisons or held in chains. The major religions of the world have long recognized this right to protection of the self, even down to the most personal level.

In bygone ages, technology couldn't keep up with the powerful's penchant to collect dossiers on masses of people. Today, the situation has reversed, and even the most ambitious practitioners of "brave new worlds," cannot keep up with what the latest spying and surveillance technologies can deliver. In 2002, the Department of Defense let the secret slip out with a verbal miscue. They called their latest effort then "Total Information Awareness" (TIA). That was too much even for a supine Congress, so the Pentagon changed the name of the program to Terrorism Information Awareness and shuffled its components around — but it was never substantively revoked.

Now new technology, as etched in the pages of *The Machine Never Blinks*, crosses all boundaries (with the exception of reading your mind, at least for now). Home, work, street, schools, public buildings, parks, beaches, and health care locales — the all-seeing eye, ear, and nose ("pumping in fragrances") and their algorithms and networks are furiously aggregating your information and misinformation about you, 24/7. Alexa — now minding tens of millions of innocents — is giving forth information while its supposed masters and mistresses lie sleeping. There are few *functioning* legal and ethical frameworks to hold accountable the creation and use of these technologies — technologies with ambitions for self-activation and self-replication.

In sports terms, the offense these machines present outruns any defense by their innovators. Hacking outraces present protections. Hacking gives nightmares to those illusionists calling for autonomous vehicles, autonomous medical devices, and autonomous weapons. Where are the defenses against cyberattacks other than the deterrent of receiving a retaliatory attack — if the cyberattacker can even be found?

Without enforceable restraints on the surveillance technology exploding in capitalistic and communistic societies, each adopting their techniques and learning from their experience (to wit: the U.S. and China), the modern players take center stage. The intruders are large corporations and government agencies, and can be any invasive institutions, from universities to unions, that see the need for giant eyes, ears, and similar detectors. These players build autocracies in their own realms, then often blend themselves into the corporate-controlled state. Crony capitalism finds a new medium of exchange — petabytes (that's thousands of terabytes) of surveillance data.

There are also the rising non-institutional, anonymous criminal predators feeding off the vulnerable. The spectacular reduction in the cost of using these technologies deprives price of its customary restraints. Note the pervasive robocalls we all receive.

Criminal ransomware has already reaped monies from two town governments in Florida, denying them access to their own data until they paid up. They paid — and they weren't the only ones. Little-known microdata brokers now feed well-known corporate vendors with what is called "Secret Surveillance Scores"[1] enabling companies to charge their customers different prices for the same products and services in the same markets — and making it more costly and difficult for those seeking housing or employment. Totally out of control. No law, no organized condemnation — just business in a different garb.

The far-seeing cautionary dystopian novels *Nineteen Eighty-Four* by George Orwell and *Brave New World* by Aldous Huxley are mere understatements when compared to contemporary control regimes. Your own body will soon become the mechanism of your surveillance — your own electronic gulag. The chips will become nano and ubiquitous. The collection and storage of your DNA data (voluntary or surreptitious), your facial profile, what you buy, who you see, who you have been near, and exactly where you are at any given moment is increasingly being conducted by machines that constantly report back to their nameless wardens.

Using Facebook, Google, et al., makes *you* the product. It induces you into history's greatest exercise of consumer complicity, empowering and enriching the giant addictors who are bent on capturing your time, your focus, and your data, while preserving the illusion of personal freedom, self-determination, and some measure of introspection or contemplation.

I find it necessary from time to time to alert people crossing streets who are oblivious to oncoming vehicles because they are immersed in their iPhones. You can imagine the frustration of street petitioners collecting signatures for democratic actions attempting to establish eye contact with all those faces looking downward at screens as they walk by. So much for horizons!

All these trends get worse as the inequality of power, wealth, and access to media tilts ever more steeply in favor of the privileged. These invasions are physical, psychological, and perpetual. Your information floats around the world in unseen hands. It does not go away or get forgotten — it remains ready to strike back again and again over years. And the perpetrators are immune to even smidgens of accountability. After the long-delayed Federal Trade Commission's pathetic enforcement action against Facebook in 2019, the company walked away with immunity from all its violations in the past. Witness the weak Congressional hearings on the doings of Facebook, Google, Amazon, and others. The solons hardly knew what to utter by way of questions, never mind any compelling follow-ups.

After the National Security Agency (NSA) and the other intelligence agencies with their unaccountable dragnet surveillance power, the most invasive surveillance innovators are the corporations associated with Silicon Valley. These firms, oblivious to boundaries, are driven to maximize profit and share price. They grow without traditional limits imposed by force of law or by any traditional consumer class opposition. They are not traditional business models with traditional profit margins with traditional pricing formulae. The people using their services can scarcely understand what's happening in the industry, and, crucially, what is gradually but relentlessly happening to themselves.

Unlike the entertainment and fast-food industries that bypass parents and market directly *to* children, these internet companies elicit a massive array of personal information directly *from* children and then sell direct access to those same children and their families to advertisers and marketers. Facebook extracts a "click-on" fine-print contract from these children, securing their agreement to give their personal information to the company, while denying them remedies. Facebook's lawyers have the effrontery to require children to affirm that they received the approval of one parent to submit to such a one-sided deal. That one example of the utter lack of corporate shame means few self-restraints on your personal information being bought and sold around the world!

How do we protect ourselves? We can all take active steps to fight back. First, absorb the history that the authors narrate here of the horrors that surveillance and spying have wreaked upon the people in passive societies. The story that follows — told in the comics format — makes this point from ancient history to now, with deep caveats. Our founding fathers, in the late 18th century, added the Fourth Amendment to our Constitution against unlawful governmental search and seizure of persons and property. They viewed this protection as critical to human freedom — the right to be left alone. Basic and brief, here is the text:

> The right of the people to be secure in their persons, houses, papers, and effects, against unreasonable searches and seizures, shall not be violated, and no Warrants shall issue, but upon probable cause, supported by Oath or affirmation, and particularly describing the place to be searched, and the persons or things to be seized.

The Fourth Amendment is just one of several sections of the Constitution which led the courts to recognize our constitutional right of privacy. The challenge is to apply and enforce this majestic right down to where the snoopers, and their insidious toys, work in darkness.

Deriving from our Constitution and several federal and state privacy laws, there are other preparations for resistance. Suing the snoopers is good for America. There is a recent lawsuit, under Illinois law, against Facebook for misuse of facial recognition technology which, reports say, could cost the company billions of dollars. American tort law includes violations of privacy and defamation as torts or wrongful injuries actionable in courts with the right to trial by jury (the Seventh Amendment).

Depending on your situation and temperament, you can disconnect from the hellfire of the internet — or at least the worst of it. Get out of the Facebook, Google, Microsoft, Amazon, Apple vortex. As much as possible, return to direct interpersonal relationships and return to cash/check transactions locally. Join consumer cooperatives that are growing in number.

Get out of the arenas of contract, fine-print servitude. Rejecting the credit-card and debit-card systems of incarceration where you lose control over your money, your privacy, your right to oppose or contest penalties, overcharges, suspensions, and damage to your credit scores that flow directly from such contract peonage. Be free to complain, to voice your grievance over rip-offs without being told how you are damaging your credit ratings, which handcuff your right to protest.

Connect with the kinds of reforms espoused by Electronic Privacy Information Center (EPIC)[2] and other citizen groups fighting surveillance capitalism. If you remain inside the gulag, demand changes in the underlying fine-print contracts. Break these chains. Press other companies to provide you with the good encryption now provided by Apple, Inc. Dissolving these contracts with fairer replacements — whether by litigation, legislation, or regulation can shake up and stall the whole repressive system to its foundations. For underneath most of the abuses is the *contract*.

If we organize and demand it, government can be our defender and protector from these corporate supremacists. That means you can organize Congress Watchdog Groups [3] Under our Constitution, controlling a majority of the 535 senators and representatives in the smallest but most powerful branch of our federal government — the legislature — can turn around the executive branch, which is, at present, largely captured. Congress has the power to make the federal agencies stand for the people and make corporations your servants, not your masters. You can empower yourself by using the federal and state freedom of information acts to pry loose files (even your own) from government agencies. Learn how in the footnotes below.[4]

The corporate bosses are not invincible. We have the votes. We can control where we spend our money by the ways we act as citizens and shoppers. Less than one percent of active, connected citizens in the 435 Congressional districts, backed by public opinion, can get it done.

Lastly, remember, our information can be either the currency of democracy or the profitable inventory for corporate coercion and government oppression. We must be stingy in what and how we give it away. *The Machine Never Blinks*, by its dedicated creators — Ivan Greenberg, Everett Patterson, and Joseph Canlas — is the educational and motivational wake-up call for the people to take back control over "The Machine" in the name of humanity and justice.

Ralph Nader is a long-time consumer advocate, a four-time presidential candidate, and author of many books, including the jolting tutorial for citizens, *The Day the Rats Vetoed Congress*, an illustrated "fable of political action" due from Fantagraphics Books in 2020. Mr. Nader has started dozens of citizen groups on multiple subjects (see nader.org). His weekly podcast is *The Ralph Nader Radio Hour* (ralphnaderradiohour.com). To sign up for his free weekly column of news and commentary via email, go to nader.org.

1 See the petition at https://www.representconsumers.org/wp-content/
    uploads/2019/06/2019.06.24-FTC-Letter-Surveillance-Scores.pdf
2 Visit the Electronic Privacy Information Center (EPIC) at https://epic.org
3 You can organize your own Congress Watchdog Group. Go to https://ratsreformcongress.org/
    for details and to apply.
4 Learn how to use federal and state freedom of information acts for your own purposes at
    https://www.citizen.org/article/freedom-of-information-clearinghouse

Introduction:
LIVING IN A SURVEILLANCE SOCIETY

Hi, my name is Iggy Stone. I've got a few things I want to talk about. We used to call this the Information Society. Things have changed dramatically within the last twenty years. It's now a Surveillance Society.

Do you ever feel like you are being watched? Today, the unprecedented monitoring of people poses a real threat to our rights, privacy, integrity...and sanity.

The watching comes in many forms. Most of us are only beginning to notice it. It is all about power and struggle--who watches and who is being watched. Big entities--government, business, and criminals--can now make every little routine visible. There is almost nowhere to hide.

Surveillance occurs at home, at work, and everywhere in between. Big new databases assemble this collected mass data to identify "dangerous" patterns and people.

Everyone is spying on everyone.

DOWNTO'

8097

How can we live with so much outside watching and tracking and datamining? How do we object to it?? It has never been as bad as it is right now.

IF YOU SEE SOMETHING ...SAY SOMETHING

Smartphones have revolutionized communications…

But they've also made most Americans vulnerable to the collection of huge amounts of their personal data--calendars, photographs, email, contact lists-- a person's entire social network.

There is another dark side. GPS tracking devices can act as an electronic geo-tag, and microphones may be activated remotely…

….to become secret listening devices. Technological advances are not always in the public's interest.

Tiny electronic tracking spy chips are attached to everyday objects. The chips use Radio Frequency Identification (RFID).

These may be fixed to car windshields acting as toll paying devices and embedded in passports, library books, work uniforms, luggage, and some consumer goods.

Chips planted beneath the skin of our dogs can access their location in case they wander off and get lost

My dog is under surveillance for his own good.

Experts predict human "chipping" will be used in the future on a much greater scale than today--a major departure from centuries of history and tradition in which free people go and do as they please without being monitored.

Do we really want to make all things traceable?

Woof.

The collection of identifying records involving the body is called

"BIOMETRICS."

Facial images. Fingerprints. Handprints. Iris scans. Tattoos. Government even wants a record of our DNA.

Doctor, don't create a record of everything you see...My tattoos are not your business.

Look, Mr. Stone, I try to protect the confidentiality of all my patients' records.

That reminds me...your employer notified me that it's time for your yearly drug test.

I don't want these records to become part of some big database.

Defeat the white man.

First developed in 1983, electronic ankle bracelets for criminal offenders are now a big part of the penal system, tracking the movements of subjects confined to house arrest.

Some have an accessory to test for alcohol or marijuana, and some even have a listening device.

More than 200,000 Americans wear a penal e-monitor on their bodies. It is better than being in jail, but electronic surveillance makes its way into the home. There may be very negative social and psychological impacts, especially for juvenile offenders.

That bracelet haunts me. If I step outside, it is going to shock me good!

CCTV can be used to observe political activity. Authorities study the live video feeds in special Command and Control Centers. They take special notice of large gatherings of people.

Look, people are assembling at Washington Square Park. I don't think a protest is planned there today.

Is it the Occupy Wall Street demonstrators?

I don't recognize anyone.

The "War on Terror" devotes significant new monitoring of Arab American Muslims in their communities.

It looks like they just got out of mosque. I see that guy we got a memo about...His beard is longer.

Maybe he's planning something.

I swear he looks just like Osama bin Laden.

Surveillance systems often depend on global positioning satellites (GPS), miles above the ground.

Unmanned spy drones fly above the clouds to identify everything in their path. While most of their deployment is overseas, law enforcement has begun to use spy aircraft at home as well.

I think that bird is tailing me!

A small drone known as the Nano Hummingbird resembles a real bird and is used for short-range reconnaissance. The mechanical bird flies around and tries to blend into the environment, with a CCTV camera and sensors embedded in it.

CHIRP CHIRP

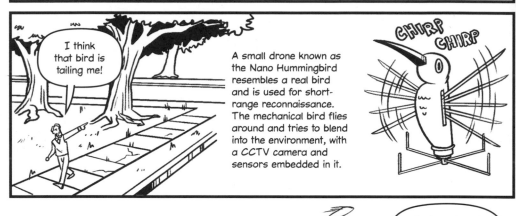

And we should worry that they'll invade our personal space, too!

Americans are increasingly buying small drones for their personal use. Some 7 million are projected to be in use in the U.S. by 2020. The Federal Aviation Administration is terrified drones will crowd the airspace and interfere with airplane traffic.

The recent media leaks by whistleblower Edward J. Snowden started a new debate in America about government surveillance versus incursions on individual privacy and civil liberties.

Snowden leaked tens of thousands of secret spy documents from the National Security Agency (NSA), revealing massive internet and cell phone surveillance of both Americans and foreigners.

Today, our most intimate private records are being indiscriminately seized in secret, without regard for whether we are actually suspected of wrongdoing. When these capabilities fall into the wrong hands, they can destroy the very freedoms that technology should be nurturing, not extinguishing. Surveillance, without regard to the rule of law or our basic human dignity, creates societies that fear free expression and dissent, the very values that make America strong.

A federal court eventually vindicated Snowden's whistleblowing by ruling that NSA surveillance needs to be reformed. The court referred to the unconstitutional "Orwellian" aspects of the NSA's unaccountable spying.

Today's high-tech monitoring finds its roots in religion, industrial relations, warfare, politics, and criminal justice.

Exploring this history offers a dazzling and disturbing look at a subject that's here to stay.

In short, Big Brother is everywhere, but this didn't all just happen yesterday....

It's been going on in one form or another since ancient times.

Throughout the long sweep of history, spying and secret infiltration have been key aspects of human existence.

One of the Western world's iconic confrontations created one of the greatest icons of subterfuge. During the Trojan War of the 12th or 13th century BCE, the greatest military conflict in Greek mythology...

...the "Trojan Horse" became the weapon that deceived an entire city...

...ended an ancient war...

Chapter 1: THE TROJAN HORSE

...and yet lives on to this day.

In one maneuver, the Greeks had immortalized spying from without and infiltration from within.

The legend of the Trojan Horse is now well known. The victim unwittingly invites a disguised foe into a protected space. Once inside, the foe launches a sneak attack.

Today, the idea has been reborn in cyberspace as computer "malware" programs. Millions of malware attacks occur every year, invading and corrupting computers and smartphones.

Computer malware presents itself as harmless, inducing the subject to install it on their computer. Once inside, it destroys existing functions or harvests them for personal data. Cyber-Trojans cause nearly eighty percent of all computer infections worldwide.

The largest known breach at a U.S. retailer was uncovered in 2007 at the T.J. Maxx and Marshalls chains, where more than ninety million credit cards were stolen over an eighteen-month period. In 2014, millions of computers at Target and Home Depot were attacked and customer credit information stolen through "memory scraping."

This modern, digital predation includes the "Red Code" worm in 2001, which managed to infect more than 350,000 Microsoft servers in a mere fourteen-hour period.

Sometimes malware worms are government-sponsored. In the case of Stuxnet in 2010, U.S. and Israeli intelligence agencies allegedly directed a computer worm at Iranian government computers to disrupt its nuclear weapons program.

Symptoms of a malware infection include "locked computers," where the victim is compelled to pay a ransom to access their own device, and "phantom messages," where phony emails or social media posts are distributed under the victim's name.

The Greeks claimed defeat and sailed away, leaving the horse at the gates of Troy.

The Greeks let it be known they had left it as an offering to the goddess Minerva, who was associated with wisdom, war, and crafts.

A horse was also the symbol of the city of Troy, so the Trojans wheeled it inside as a victory trophy.

They paid little attention to Sinon, the solitary soldier accompanying it, who claimed he had been abandoned by the departing force.

According to the *Aeneid*, a single Trojan leader--the high priest Laocoon--warned against accepting the horse as a gift.

O unhappy citizens, what madness! Do you think the enemy has sailed away? Or do you think any Greek gifts free of treachery?

Laocoon threw a great spear into the Horse's belly, but the hidden Greek soldiers inside stood firm.

Today, few people resist the use of electronic technology despite the naysayers, who correctly warn of threats from secret attacks.

The anti-virus pioneer Symantec admits that scanning software to detect malware is ineffective in almost half of all secret attacks.

In South Korea, the mass attack by the Trojan Horse virus "Hastati" raged across numerous institutions, from banks to TV stations, rendering thousands of computers unusable. It was activated on March 20, 2013, at 2:00 pm.

It overwrote computer files to make data unrecoverable. Hacktivists in North Korea likely were responsible for this covert espionage campaign, which became known as Operation Troy.

The hacktivists also left a calling card a day after the attacks--web pop-up messages, claiming the "New Romanic Cyber Army Team" had been responsible.

As Troy slept, the Greek warriors exited the Horse's belly by sliding down a rope.

The Greek warriors then opened the city's gates to an invading army, headed by the military leader Pyrrhus.

Today, the gates are open to secret computer invasions, in part because of popular fatigue. According to a recent study, about a third of computer users opt to click through warnings that a Web page is not secure. Even after company data breaches, many people fail to change their account passwords for their own protection.

IT professionals identify popular data breach fatigue, "a feeling of utter weariness and discontent resulting from the occurrence of multiple cyber attacks within a short period of time."

Yet, despite the ubiquity of malware, there is little popular pushback against electronic technology.

Government infrastructure is even more dependent on this technology...and attacks such as Trojan Hastati and Stuxnet demonstrate their continued vulnerability.

The Greek army destroyed Troy... setting it on fire.

In another malware attack in 2012, Iran launched its own online attacks against dozens of American internet banking sites, partly as retaliation for Stuxnet. Security experts likened the attacks to a pack of fire-breathing Godzillas.

When governments use malware as a weapon, they often resort to "denial of service" attacks by directing a large volume of traffic to a site until it collapses. When financial institutions are targeted, individual accounts usually are not breached and customers' money rarely is stolen.

Spying from without and infiltration from within: The ancient Greeks' story forms an early precedent to today's surveillance society. Unfortunately, Trojan Horses have become a major headache that we face today.

Chapter 2: THE BIBLE'S SPIES

In both the Old and New Testaments of the Bible, there are lessons in watching, spying, and informing that have become firmly established as tenets of modern civilization.

These ideas have entered society through religion for many generations of people. The uniting theme is that an omni-present force watches over individuals and society. A surveilling gaze makes all things visible--and is a thing to be completely accepted...

...even asked for regularly, through prayer.

Believers live with the certainty that *God* will keep them safe and guide them. In the Psalms (121:3), we are told: "He will not let your foot slip--he who watches over you will not slumber."

With this assurance, there is also a tacit agreement that *God* watches over them at all times; that they are never hidden from the Lord's gaze. According to Psalm 139, "Lord, thou hast searched me out and known me...and spiest out all my ways."

Genesis 28:15 assumes the perspective of *God*, saying: "I am with you and will watch over you wherever you go... I will not leave you until I have done what I have promised you."

God knows my every step.

Nothing is hidden from Him.

This watchfulness is visualized with repeated images of the eyes of God.

"For the eyes of the Lord are on the righteous and His ears are attentive to their prayer."
--Psalm 34:15

"And there is no creature hidden from His sight, but all are naked and exposed to the eyes of Him..."
--Hebrews 4:13

"For the eyes of the Lord range throughout the Earth."
--2 Chronicles 16:9

"Does he not see my ways and count my every step..."
--Job 31:4

BEEP

"You discern my going out and lying down; you are familiar with all my ways."--Psalm 139:3

We love our angels--these ministering spirits and perfect celestial beings. They help God watch over us.

We are reassured that God "will order his angels to protect you in all you do" (Psalm 91:11). The Guardian Angel acts as a personal guardian, but more specifically as an agent of God enforcing his watchfulness.

The angel also serves a ministering role. "Then the devil left him, and angels came and began ministering to his needs" (Matthew 4:11).

The presence of angels encourages good hospitality. "Do not neglect to show hospitality to strangers, for thereby some have entertained angels unawares" (Hebrews 13:2).

There are dozens of references to angels in both the Old and New Testaments. Though they may be described in the form of a human body, they are generally understood as immaterial "spirits," existing above man.

Recent times have seen widespread discussion and fascination with angels, even in the secular world. Some call it "Angelmania."

Much of this fascination is only loosely tied to scripture. Polls show that about half of American adults believe a guardian angel is active in their lives to protect them.

Angels appear frequently in pop songs, movies, and television as icons of the miraculous.

CHARLIE'S ANGELS

PARADISE LOST

Christian mythology hints at a dark obverse to this reassuring picture in the figure of the fallen angel, the rebel against God. This negative view complicates the notion of surveillance in the popular imagination.

17

The Old Testament talks about "spying out the land." It actually refers to military reconnaissance.

God had promised the Israelites they would conquer the land of Canaan. This phrase meant that spies needed to scout the Promised Land for intelligence before planning an invasion.

Moses organized a spying operation, known as the Twelve Spies, while the Israelites wandered in the desert of Paran. These spies secretly entered Canaan to gauge the strength of the opposition.

See what the land is like and whether the people who live there are strong or weak, few or many.

Ten of the spies falsely reported Canaan was too fortified for them to challenge. Only two, Joshua and Caleb, said it was time to attack.

So Moses and the Israelites would remain settled in the desert. Joshua would have his turn after Moses died forty years later.

After the death of Moses, Joshua became the leader of the tribes of Israel.

Before long, he sent his own two spies into Canaan to gather information firsthand, to prepare for an invasion.

Go and look over the land.

The Israelite spies gathered intelligence in the city of Jericho from a local woman who sheltered them.

I can tell you the city is weak--but when you attack, spare my family.

The two spies, now back in the desert, reported to Joshua that the time had come:

The Lord has surely given the whole land into our hands... all the people are melting in fear because of us!

The intelligence inspired Joshua to mobilize a force of about 40,000 for the invasion. Without the spying operation, there might not have been an invasion.

Interestingly, the Bible takes a different view of surveillance conducted between ordinary citizens. In the Old Testament, we learn--"Whoever meddles in a quarrel not his own is like one who takes a passing dog by the ears" (Proverbs 26:17).

Stay out of my affairs! For the Bible instructs one "to aspire to live quietly, and to mind your own affairs...as we instructed you" (1 Thessalonians 4:11).

In the New Testament, spying in the affairs of other people is equated with murder and theft. "If you suffer, it should not be as a murderer or thief or any other kind of criminal, or even as a meddler" (1 Peter 4:15).

There is disapproval of those "who sneaked in to spy upon our freedom" (Galatians 2:4).

People shouldn't snoop into the personal lives of others, including enemies. Timothy 5:13 refers to "gossips and busybodies, saying what they should not."

Love thy neighbor...don't spy on them.

In short, the Bible considers God's gaze to be good, but seems to consider it a wholly different matter for ordinary people to engage in spying. The act of watching over another is represented as the privilege of a higher authority, which imposes discipline with omnipresent eyes.

In the Passion story, Judas Iscariot approached the chief priests and asked if he should arrange for Jesus to be apprehended.

"So they counted out for him thirty silver coins. From then on Judas watched for an opportunity to hand him over." Jesus's friend and disciple had become a paid informer...a person who named names for the government. Ever since, the name "Judas" has become synonymous with "betrayer."

On the night of the Last Supper, Judas's kiss identified the rabble-rouser Jesus to the arresting Roman authorities in the garden of Gethsemane.

The story has been interpreted in different ways--betrayal between individuals, but also betrayal involving the power of the state.

Modern references to Judas convey a betrayal of a confidence or a person's privacy.

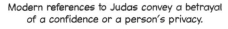

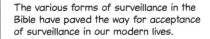

The various forms of surveillance in the Bible have paved the way for acceptance of surveillance in our modern lives.

Someone may peep through a "Judas hole." A "Judas window" often means a two-way mirror.

The Bible's surveillance lessons need to be better recognized for their larger impact, since they continue to influence millions of people around the world.

The all-seeing gaze of God, too, has parallels in law, as government develops new mechanisms for monitoring while claiming higher authority which citizens are told to respect.

Voyeurism is defined as the act of secretly watching another.

It derives from curiosity, a natural human instinct, but in practice it usually constitutes an invasion of someone else's privacy.

Chapter 3: PEEPING TOM

The "Peeping Tom" is considered to be a social deviant, transgressing normal and acceptable behavior.

This close observer is unwelcome. As the poet W.H. Auden has said: "Peeping Toms/are never praised, like novelists or bird watchers,/for their keenness of observation."

Modern-day busybodies should restrict their gazes to respect the dignity and worth of other people.

The expression "Peeping Tom" dates to the legend of Lady Godiva of the 11th century.

Lady Godiva was a devout English noblewoman with a big heart, professing concern for the poor. She was married to Leofric, Earl of Mercia, who placed heavy taxes on the people of Coventry.

Not only we, that prate
of rights and wrongs,
have loved the people well,

And loathed to see them
overtax'd: but she

Did more, and underwent,
and overcame,

The woman of a thousand
summers back.

The poetry of Alfred Lord Tennyson helped make her story famous.

Godiva appealed to her husband to lessen the citizens' tax burden. Tennyson's words immortalized what happened next.

She told him of their tears,
And pray'd him, "If they pay
this tax, they starve."

Whereat he stared,
replying, half-amazed,
"You would not let your
little finger ache
For such as these?" —
"But I would die,"
said she.

Leofric ordered the townspeople to remain indoors. They were told to shut their windows during *Godiva's* ride to preserve her honor. All did...

...except one.

Alas, a tailor named Tom disobeyed. He "peeped" at *Godiva* through the window of his shop.

Legend says Tom was immediately struck blind.

The contemporary Peeping Tom has an affinity with eavesdropping. It can be considered a form of spying.

In the U.S., video voyeurism is often viewed as a crime. Two-way mirrors and peepholes, especially when used to invade someone's sexual privacy, have long been considered an unlawful offense.

But *some* popular peeping has become acceptable.

In the *case* of reality television, the Peeping Tom concept wins with mass audience approval. The key issue is consent--whether a person gives approval to be watched.

In 1791, the English philosopher Jeremy Bentham designed a circular architectural structure called the Panopticon (literally meaning "all-seeing"). It was conceived as a building with a large tower in the center, manned by a watchman at the top who looks out and monitors subjects residing along the perimeter.

Chapter 4: THE PANOPTICON

It was thought of as an ideal new design for prisons and madhouses.

The watchman could see everyone--and see them all the time. But the watched would never be able to know when they were being observed.

Bentham thought the subjects of this constant monitoring would internalize a feeling of "self-surveillance," providing a further way to control and dominate them.

He said the Pantopticon provided "a new mode of obtaining power of mind over mind." In Bentham's view, it served as a peaceful way to monitor and subdue the ne'er-do-wells in society.

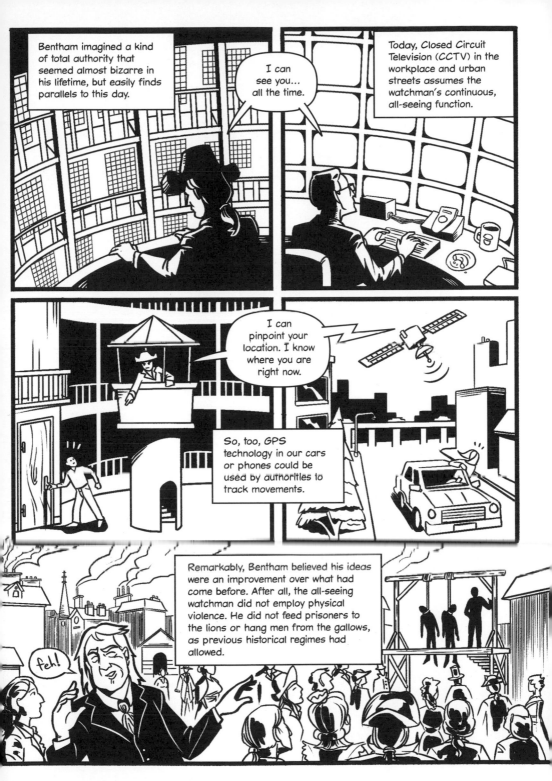

Bentham imagined a kind of total authority that seemed almost bizarre in his lifetime, but easily finds parallels to this day.

I can see you... all the time.

Today, Closed Circuit Television (CCTV) in the workplace and urban streets assumes the watchman's continuous, all-seeing function.

I can pinpoint your location. I know where you are right now.

So, too, GPS technology in our cars or phones could be used by authorities to track movements.

Remarkably, Bentham believed his ideas were an improvement over what had come before. After all, the all-seeing watchman did not employ physical violence. He did not feed prisoners to the lions or hang men from the gallows, as previous historical regimes had allowed.

feh!

The modern French philosopher Michel Foucault famously analyzed Bentham's work in the 1975 book *DISCIPLINE AND PUNISH*.

Foucault wrote: "The Panopticon must not be understood as a dream building; it is the diagram of a mechanism of power reduced to its ideal."

Foucault's interest in systems of power led him to conclude that modern authorities discipline and police populations in ways that often appear invisible, but are known to the general public.

He developed a new vocabulary to analyze how surveillance is imposed on the general population.

institution of controls

self-surveillant

technological trajectories

biopolitics

visual-spatial contingency

"The eye sees all..."

"visible is vulnerable..."

"erosion of the subjective self..."

"permanent visibility is dangerous..."

Foucault understood that official governmental surveillance could be a powerful force that eroded the integrity and autonomy of the individual.

In addition to being an architectural form, Bentham had intended the Panopticon to be viewed as an abstract "figure of political technology" to be used in hierarchical relationships to assert power.

Foucault went further. His philosophical ruminations waxed far and wide about the Panopticon and the positions of both seeing and being watched. Modern authorities would accept these ideas-- and use surveillance for social control.

Of course, Bentham and Foucault have critics. In real life, total surveillance systems are difficult for authorities to impose. And people do not have to be passive victims.

Some people don't care about being watched, saying they have nothing to hide. People also may simply become detached from the watcher's values. They don't care what authorities do. These are attitudes that can't be controlled.

It's said that hearing, touching, and smelling are just as important as seeing. These senses are beyond the Panopticon's reach.

BONG·
BONG·

Bentham could never convince authorities--whether in Ireland, France, or England--to build an experimental Panopticon prison.

He died in 1832. In his will, he requested that his body be dissected as part of a public anatomy lecture.

I can see every detail...

I feel like a Peeping Tom.

After the dissection, Bentham had his skeleton and head preserved and stored in a wooden cabinet called the "Auto-icon" and placed on public display.

JEREMY BENTHAM

Although Bentham's ideas about ever-present watching by authorities were not realized in his lifetime, they have influenced many subsequent generations of thinkers and policy makers.

Before the Civil War, the American South had a flourishing economy based in agriculture and the plantation system. The region generated vast wealth with a variety of profitable cash crops, such as cotton, tobacco, indigo, rice, and sugar cane.

Many people benefitted from the Southern way of life. A wealthy class of planters, as well as others who owned farms, enjoyed a relatively high standard of living.

But the South also was home to a brutal system of slavery that helped create that wealth and deprived African Americans of basic freedoms and human dignity.

Chapter 5: SLAVERY AND SURVEILLANCE

Slaves were first brought from Africa to the Americas in the 1600s in ships, where they were shackled and stacked like wood in the vessels' holds, anticipating their long history of suffering and oppression in America.

Once in America, they and their children were considered property and had no civil rights under the law to protect them against abuse by their owners.

Slavery provided a cheap labor system for Southerners. Many slaves picked cotton, the largest crop in the South.

Southern cotton became the chief raw material for textiles made in America and also was shipped overseas for sale in Europe. A typical slave picked several hundred pounds of cotton every day.

By 1860, the dawn of the Civil War, about 4 million slaves resided in the South. Almost one-quarter of white Southern households owned slaves, and many others held ambitions to acquire them.

Owners provided slaves a barely sustainable life. There were crowded living quarters in one- or two-room wood cabins with dirt floors. The owners gave them a meager diet and only a few sets of clothes for each season. A slave was lucky to own more than one pair of shoes.

These patrols, riding on horseback, were called "beat companies" since they often assaulted slaves whether or not they held travel passes. The companies served as an instrument to preserve white dominance.

Boy, where you going?

But I have a pass. Here...Unhh!

WHACK!

Quiet, boy!

The beat companies sometimes were paid by local governments and might include members of the militia and army. They often received benefits for their service, in addition to pay, such as being exempt from local taxes.

Many of these patrollers came from low-income backgrounds and did not themselves own slaves. But serving in beat companies connected them in brutal ways to the preservation of the slave system and reinforced a racial ideology that helped unite white society.

Some slaves who went off the plantation never returned. They became fugitives. They lived like bandits, hiding from the beat companies and other authorities.

It was easier for runaway slaves to reach the North and gain freedom if they knew how to read. Literate slaves could better navigate their journey to freedom by reading signs and other materials. They also might forge travel documents. They became information outlaws by acquiring knowledge that whites hoped to deny them.

I've got to make it to Philadelphia. I hope I don't get caught. I can't go back. I won't be a slave any longer.

Besides wanted posters, hundreds of advertisements appeared in Southern newspapers offering rewards for the return of runaway slaves.

WANTED
NEGROE MAN
SHORT, ABOUT 30 YEARS OLD
GOES BY NAME HARRY
OWNER: RALPH ARNOLD

Since literacy aided African Americans' mobility and independence, Southern states passed laws criminalizing any effort by them to learn to read or write. Whites, too, faced criminal penalties if they helped African Americans become literate or move freely in the South.

Slave rebellions in the South, while not very common, impacted white attitudes and served as an outlet for black rage and strivings toward freedom. In the aftermath of such rebellions, Southern state legislatures often passed new laws to assert more control over the slavery system.

A major slave uprising occurred in 1739 near Charleston, South Carolina, called the Stono Rebellion. About a hundred slaves raided the master's house and killed twenty whites.

Been down too long. Kill the slave master!

He sold two of my children.

The slaves stole guns and knives, which they otherwise were forbidden to own.

Put down your weapon, boy. It's time to go back to work.

It's time for you to go to hell.

The legislature in South Carolina responded to the Stono Rebellion by passing the Negro Act, which punished slaves in new ways. The Act prohibited slaves from growing their own food, assembling in groups, or learning to write. It restricted the ability of slaves to leave the plantation.

Moreover, slave owners now needed legislative approval to free any of their slaves. This attempt to restrict manumission reflected white fears that the presence of free blacks encouraged the enslaved to rebel.

But Southern surveillance and control methods to maintain law and order over African Americans eventually failed, as the nation was compelled to engage in a bloody civil war to dissolve the system of slavery.

Chapter 6: THE INDUSTRIAL AGE

New classes of workers and bosses formed during the beginning of the Industrial Age. The invention of fast-paced machinery changed the nature of work.

Thousands of poor immigrants from Europe flooded into American cities, looking for jobs in factories and small workshops.

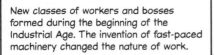

The upper class "better sort" wanted to control the lower class "mobs."

Hi there, common men. Reading the newspaper, are you? I'm hiring today.

Come along now, if you want to work.

The factory job was every day but Sunday, sunrise to sunset.

You've got to follow all of my rules-- everything I say.

Factories dramatically increased the production of goods. Many more people could afford to buy these new goods because they were sold at cheaper prices than goods made by craftsmen.

But the work was very demanding.

As industrialization continued to spread, official efforts to track the public increased in order to maintain law and order and reduce conflict in society.

Make sure we establish a full record on this ne'er-do-well.

He's sure to get in trouble again.

In 1912, *The New York Times* declared: "The unidentified American--we find him everywhere trouble is."

After the invention of photography, the New York Police Department pioneered a "Rogues' Gallery"--photo albums of criminals for the public to inspect. It was one of the first assemblages of police files on the American people.

In the early 1900s, police established fingerprinting to create more detailed records on suspects.

I remember arresting him for disorderly conduct. He swung at me. Move on...

By assuming the "unidentified American" posed a danger, American leaders began to follow a path towards multiple surveillance methods for social control.

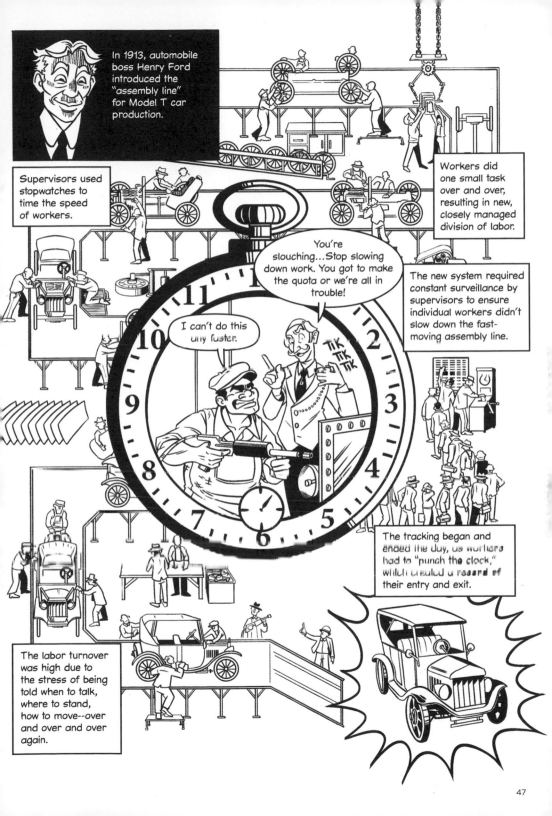

Management began to monitor their workforces with labor spies, who secretly watched the employees.

Some workers were recruited, but outside spies also were placed in the workforce.

By the 1920s, about 200,000 labor spies were employed in American industry.

I heard a rumor management wants to cut our wages by 15 percent.

They can't do that. It's not fair. I won't be able to feed my family!

We should go out on strike!

As unionization, encouraged by New Deal policies, gained power during the 1930s, firms aimed their hired spies at employees with progressive political views.

Until the establishment of the National Labor Relations Board provided a measure of accountability in the hiring and firing process, striking was a fireable offense...

...and sometimes, even a criminal one. Bosses often called in the city police to bust strikes by arresting workers.

One way or another, spies undermined their work peers, including dooming their jobs if management wanted to bust their workers.

During World War II, as men left to fight in Europe, many women took jobs in heavy industry for the first time. They experienced surveillance like the men, but sometimes also had to contend with unwanted sexual harassment.

In the 21st century, more than a third of all workplaces have "electronic eyes"...also known as Closed Circuit Television or CCTV.

In some workplaces, employee ID cards are fitted with GPS tracking devices.

Management knows where all their employees are at any given time; when they take a bathroom or coffee break, and for how long.

Bosses, citing the need to have employees use their phones for official business only, may record conversations. The wiretapping of telephones occurs in the workplace more than anywhere else in society.

Management can restrict, track, and record the internet use of their employees. Many employers check employee social media contacts, such as Facebook.

Since management owns the machines, they have the legal right to surveil them.

Chapter 7: THE FIRST RED SCARE

In 1914, war broke out all over Europe. In 1917, Communists in Russia triumphed in the Bolshevik Revolution.

As the 20th century began in tumult, Americans demonstrated their opinions by marching in the streets.

LET THERE BE

NO WAR

Some opposed the war because they felt the wealthy few were making decisions for the unwealthy many.

No to the rich man's war!

RESIST CON-SCRIPTION

Some opposed the war because they felt the true battles were at home.

We deserve the right to vote!

WE DEMAND LIBERTY

VOTES FOR WOMEN

Some were among the twenty-four million immigrants who had resettled in America within just twenty-five years.

The tsars killed my family! Socialism will save Russia and America, too!

All of a sudden, the U.S. government became worried about the political loyalties of the American people. A new era of government surveillance in domestic politics had begun.

We need to make the world safe for democracy.

President Woodrow Wilson sought a declaration of war from the U.S. Congress to fight the Axis Powers--Germany, Austria-Hungary, and Turkey.

But in his declaration, Wilson cast a wider net for domestic enemies.

If there should be disloyalty--

--it will be dealt with a firm hand of repression.

Wilson and the U.S. Congress held little tolerance for anti-war opinion. Wilson issued an executive order allowing for the censorship of communications by mail, cable, radio or other means of transmission.

The U.S. Congress passed a series of laws to clamp down on dissent and to arrest and deport radicals--the Espionage Act (1917)...the Alien Act (1918)...the Sedition Act (1918).

These laws proved to be a very heavy-handed attempt to enforce conformity about the war and to undermine alternative views. As critics of U.S. policy became framed as mortal enemies, the civil liberties of Americans came under severe attack.

The Alien Act empowered the government to deport hundreds of immigrants, and the Sedition Act was used to convict more than 2,000 people for opposing the war.

This included national Socialist leader Eugene V. Debs, who was arrested after giving an anti-war speech in Dayton, Ohio.

It is extremely dangerous to exercise the constitutional right of free speech in a country fighting to make democracy safe in the world.

After being sentenced to a ten-year prison term, Debs said: "I am opposing a social order in which it is possible for one man who does absolutely nothing that is useful to amass a fortune of hundreds of millions of dollars, while millions of men and women who work all the days of their lives secure barely enough for a wretched existence."

The government intensified its campaign against anti-war, left-wing radicals. In 1917, it arrested, and later deported, Anarchist leader Emma Goldman. Goldman had emerged as a very popular speaker, championing a variety of causes including birth control, free speech, and anti-militarism.

She argued that American intervention in World War I would serve to protect "the vilest plutocracy on the face of the earth." She also supported military draft resistance in the *Alarm*, a radical newspaper.

To charge people with having conspired to do something, which they have been engaged in doing most of their lives, namely their campaign against war, militarism, and conscription as contrary to the best interests of humanity, is an insult to human intelligence.

The publicized arrests of Debs and Goldman helped pave the way for government attacks against lesser-known people and their followers. A new era of surveillance and repression in American politics had taken hold.

Within the U.S. Justice Department, the newly established Bureau of Investigation (BOI), the precursor to the FBI, began to spy on radical groups. It infiltrated different left-wing organizations to learn about their political activities and to identify their members.

On June 2, 1919, radical anarchists set off bombs in nine American cities. The home of U.S. Attorney General A. Mitchell Palmer was targeted. A bomb also went off on Wall St. in Manhattan.

The success of Communists in Russia increased government surveillance in America. Within a short period, the government's political files on radicals swelled to more than 200,000.

In response to the bombings, the BOI undertook a "vigorous and comprehensive" investigation of anarchists, Communists, and other "kindred" agitators.

A young J. Edgar Hoover, later the long-time director of the FBI, led the new special Radical Division within the Justice Department to coordinate political surveillance. Hoover hired a force of 40 readers to monitor as many as 625 radical publications. He believed the secret collection of political intelligence was vital to fight the threat posed by radicalism.

Hoover boasted about the new intelligence system: "At a moment's notice a card upon an individual, organization, or a general society existing in any part of the country can be obtained and a brief resume found on the card requested."

As World War I ended, the nation was gripped with social and political turmoil. In 1919, about four million American workers went out on strike demanding better working conditions.

In Seattle, about 35,000 shipyard workers participated in a strike.

Shut down the city. Seattle is ours! We want freedom in the workplace.

ON STRIKE

In Montana, coal miners went on strike in the countryside.

I can hardly breathe. That deadly dust is killing me!

City police officers organized a strike in Boston.

We want a pay raise. No cuts. We demand it. You gotta pay more for good law and order.

Some big corporate employers, such as Carnegie Steel, began to fingerprint and register their workers. Critics pointed out that registration could lead to blacklists.

In Cleveland, cabbies went on strike to protest being fingerprinted.

WE ARE NOT CRIMINALS

NO FINGERPRINTING

UNIONIZE

The federal government believed these strikes and other protests were the work of anti-American Communists. The new spying on radicals helped prepare the way for a crackdown on political groups. Thus began the Palmer Raids.

On Jan. 2, 1920, federal agents raided Communist meetings in 33 cities, arresting more than 6,000 people. These arrests were coordinated by federal agents who had infiltrated many of these groups pretending to be radicals.

The BOI used dubious investigation techniques-- illegal searches, warrantless arrests, agents provocateurs, and coerced confessions.

Despite such abuse of power, the popular press celebrated the Palmer Raids for containing plans for revolution in America.

Overall, the government's Red Scare campaign significantly weakened the power of progressive political movements across the nation.

In response to wartime repression, in 1918 the American Civil Liberties Union (ACLU) was formed. The ACLU took a leading role in defending the legal rights of people persecuted by the government. Before long, Hoover and the BOI began to spy on it.

JAN 3, 1920

PALMER NABS REDS!

ACLU

Racial conflict plagued the nation as well. The summer of 1919 became known as the Red Summer--red for blood. Race riots broke out in twenty-six American cities. In most cases, the riots erupted when black Americans resisted white racial violence.

One of the biggest riots took place in Chicago. It began when a white youth at a beach threw a rock at an African American youth and hit him in the head, killing him.

Anxiety crested in official government circles. The U.S. Justice Department erroneously believed that the riots were the work of radicals fomenting trouble. As a result, federal agents increased surveillance of African American leaders and their organizations.

It's the Communists' fault. Black Americans rarely resist--someone's manipulating them. We have to find out if the Communists are dominating their organizations and which leaders are advocating this insurrection.

Let's track black newspapers to see which people are disloyal and are inciting violence.

DEPARTMENT OF JUSTICE

Officials began to question the loyalty of African Americans simply because they had fought back against white violence. The government refused to view them as full citizens with legitimate concerns about racism and their unjust treatment in society.

The government's domestic Red Scare campaign continued through the 1920s. The surveillance of political activity became a permanent feature of the American government.

The government said it was looking to combat anti-American "subversion." It did not care if its political investigations invaded a subject's privacy.

Officials such as J. Edgar Hoover turned the Red Scare into a crusade. The government's surveillance machinery tracked a rapidly growing list of political suspects.

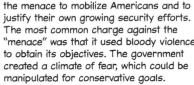

The Red Scare gave rise to the idea of a political "menace." Government sought to identify, expose, and prosecute that menace in the belief that preserving the American Way of Life depended on it.

Political leaders popularized the idea of the menace to mobilize Americans and to justify their own growing security efforts. The most common charge against the "menace" was that it used bloody violence to obtain its objectives. The government created a climate of fear, which could be manipulated for conservative goals.

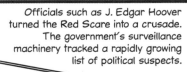

Critics of government spying called it an infringement of First Amendment rights of free speech and assembly. They also pointed out that government surveillance methods violated the Fourth Amendment protection against "unreasonable searches and seizures."

The right to protest and challenge the government is a fundamental tenet of a democratic society.

Founded in 1908, the FBI is the supreme law enforcement agency in the U.S. J. Edgar Hoover became its iron-fisted director in 1924 and served until his death nearly forty-eight years later in 1972.

Hoover was a larger-than-life political figure. He kept power so long by intimidating both his friends and enemies, including presidents, by collecting intelligence on them. The Bureau used information as a weapon.

Hoover died in his sleep of natural causes on May 2, 1972. What was he dreaming that night?

Chapter 8: HOOVER'S DREAM

I never got to be President. But...the Presidents always feared me

Why couldn't I get close to a woman?

The liberals still hate me. But we beat those damn Communists. Only that matters.

Hoover's long career occurred under the shadow of the Cold War against the Soviet Union and its allies. He interpreted the Cold War as a crusade and felt empowered to spy on anyone in America in order to fight the Communist threat.

Few outside the FBI knew the broad scope of the Bureau's spying. Hoover's FBI kept secret political files on several million Americans. Only a very small number were actual Communists.

60

For more than a decade, the Bureau watched the Reverend Martin Luther King, Jr. very closely. As King traveled around the South promoting civil rights, his government shadow kept apace. Hoover personally detested the civil rights leader. In a secret memo to other agents, he declared King "a tom-cat with obsessive degenerate sexual urges."

We have to neutralize him.

I understand, but that means bugging a dozen hotel rooms!

Just get it done.

Regarding the blacks...we must promote for them a different, more moderate leader.

How many undercover informers are spying on King?

It's substantial. And what they've found...

Just before King won the Nobel Peace Prize in 1964, Hoover's campaign against him peaked in public and in private. While Hoover called King "the most notorious liar in the nation" in a statement to journalists, his lieutenants at the FBI were sending King an anonymous letter suggesting he commit suicide to avoid having his extra-marital affairs exposed.

In 1967, the FBI started a major surveillance and counterinsurgency program against black civil rights and black power groups as part of COINTELPRO (Counter Intelligence Program). Thousands of people were put under surveillance. Just as King's legacy would live on, so would the legacy of Hoover's public and private campaigns against him.

During the late 1960s and early 1970s, President Richard Nixon directed his people at the White House to spy on Americans independently of the efforts of the FBI. Nixon matched Hoover in spying and dirty tricks to advance conservative political goals.

Look, Dick, only my people are supposed to spy on Americans. This is the FBI's work, damn it, and you've got to cut your people off at the knees.

You've got to trust me.

Nixon had recruited former government intelligence officials into a special intelligence unit called the "plumbers." Nixon's men tried to sabotage political opponents. The President kept an "enemies list" of people to target.

I hate those liberals as much as you. Leave the spying to me.

After his death, Hoover's personal secretary burned thousands of pages of his secret files. Hoover had instructed her to destroy this material to keep his secrets forever secret.

In 1975, the Bureau said it held six million political dossiers on Americans.

After Hoover died, he was given a state funeral at the National Presbyterian Church in Washington, DC. The funeral services were broadcast on national radio and television. President Nixon said in a eulogy:

"The profound principles associated with his name will not fade away. Rather, I would predict that in the time ahead those principles of respect for law, order, and justice will come to govern our national life more completely than ever before. Because the trend of permissiveness in this country, a trend which Edgar Hoover fought against all his life, a trend which was dangerously eroding our national heritage as a law-abiding people, is now being reversed."

A few months after the funeral, the U.S. Congress honored Hoover by naming the FBI headquarters building in Washington after him.

But within a few years, the Congress would turn a very critical eye on his tenure as director, as shocking revelations were made public about the FBI's broad attack on civil liberties conducted over the years.

In 1975 and 1976, the U.S. Congress held several dozen hearings on FBI abuse of power. Hoover's death would lead to reform of FBI spying.

You didn't have the authority to open mail, wiretap phones, or conduct break-ins.

No one said it *wasn't* okay. We did what we had to do to protect national security.

Why didn't you ask for legal warrants to carry out these activities?

We didn't follow that route because we assumed Congress knew what we were doing. Director Hoover had a tremendous amount of support in the Congress.

No one here sanctioned such vigilante activities, which made a mockery of the First Amendment.

Helen, tell the Senator I may have a file on him. He might like to see it.

Don't I got the Congress in my pocket?

The Washington Post

FBI BROKE THE LAW FOR YEARS

As journalist Tim Weiner has written, "Every fingerprint that's on file, every camera that looks over your shoulder as you're walking down the street in New York or London, every time you go through an airport and they get your biometric data from your eyeballs, that is the world that J. Edgar Hoover invented."

During the late 1940s and early 1950s, the U.S. government created a high level of fear by exaggerating the threat posed by *Communism* within America. The Attorney General compiled a list of more than six hundred allegedly "subversive" organizations suspected of undermining the U.S. government.

It led a hunt for alleged political radicals, who were viewed as mortal enemies. No one was above suspicion.

Many innocent people fell victim to unfounded accusations. Some were compelled to testify before Congress about their politics. The government also conducted loyalty investigations of thousands of federal employees. This included the purging of all people labeled "homosexuals," who were fired from their jobs. A *Lavender Scare* intersected with the Red Scare.

An estimated ten thousand people lost their jobs due to a "blacklist."

Political surveillance reached new heights. The FBI opened files on tens of thousands of people. Surveillance followed Americans in their daily lives via bugged phones, opened mail, physical tails, and some break-ins of homes and offices. The government said break-ins were needed to gather intelligence.

Official "scare" politics discouraged the public from engaging in political activity criticizing their own government.

Chapter 9: THE SECOND RED SCARE

The U.S. Congress took the lead in fueling the Red Scare.

Senator Joseph McCarthy of Wisconsin spread misinformation that Communist spies infiltrated not only the federal government but many other American institutions.

Congressman Richard M. Nixon of California championed the anti-Communist crusade before the House UnAmerican Activities Committee (HUAC). The Committee held hundreds of sensational hearings to expose alleged Communist influence in Hollywood, the media, educational and religious institutions, and labor unions.

Have you ever been a Communist?

Our surveillance records indicate you attended a meeting.

Are you a loyal American?

My politics aren't your business. I always obey the law. The First Amendment of the Constitution says government shall not inhibit free speech. These hearings are inhibiting speech.

I have a surveillance file on you. If you do not answer, you will be held in contempt. You could go to prison. Your silence indicates guilt.

I will not participate in this witch hunt. It is my Fifth Amendment right to remain silent. That is all I have to say.

The Red Scare came to the Hollywood film industry earlier than many other areas of American life because of the importance of movies in popular culture. HUAC first targeted Hollywood with loyalty hearings in 1947. It searched for Communists among actors, actresses, directors, and writers.

Many loyal Americans outraged by the Red Scare believed it undermined American values and traditions. Famous stars spoke out against HUAC--Humphrey Bogart, Lauren Bacall, Gene Kelly, Lucille Ball, Henry Fonda, Katherine Hepburn, Groucho Marx, and Frank Sinatra.

In the case of the "Hollywood Ten," ten witnesses who testified before HUAC were sent to prison for refusing to cooperate.

The actor Ronald Reagan enthusiastically promoted the government's crusade. Reagan, the future American president, headed the Screen Actors Guild and become a "friendly" HUAC witness against radicals.

My name is Bonzo. I'm not a Communist. I never attended a meeting.

Actor John Wayne headed a conservative patriotic group, the Motion Picture Alliance for the Preservation of American Ideals. He said in 1950, "We did not make 'Hollywood' and 'Reds' synonymous--the Communists, their fellow travelers, and their dupes did that damaging job."

In 1951, he told followers: "Our Red foes even went so far as to threaten to throw acid in the faces of myself and some other stars."

The FBI carried out several hundred "black bag jobs"--break-ins of offices and homes to gather political information. These burglaries were illegal because no prior judicial authorization was obtained.

I hit the jackpot. I just found a socialist membership list.

Our time is short. We've got only thirty-five minutes to plant a listening device and get out of here.

I put the bug under the desk drawer. No one will notice it.

I wonder what these people will say about their future plans.

I doubt they'll realize their phone is wiretapped.

Maybe we can find out where they get their money and how they are successful in recruiting people to their cause.

PEOPLE
BEFORE
PROFITS

The surveillance included undercover government agents and their recruits secretly infiltrating political groups. The spies participated in membership meetings and even tried to become leaders within targeted groups.

We want you to circulate within the socialist movement in New York City. You will join a socialist group and blend in.

Should I use my real name?

Yes. There is no need for an alias. There is very little chance that your undercover role will be blown.

I'm supposed to take notes on the people I meet and write down all the names of people at political meetings?

Yes. We will give you some literature to read on what they believe and the language they use. You have to learn how to interact effectively with them.

How often do I report back to you?

Once a week, unless something comes up that we need to know about. You'll also write a monthly report for us.

We want you to get close to the leaders. Become their friends and then tell us everything you can about them.

You are doing a patriotic service for your nation.

As a result of government repression, membership in radical groups declined. The Red Scare drove many people away from political activity.

It's too dangerous to be active in Left politics these days.

No kidding! My friend lost his job.

I'm a writer. I'm afraid of the blacklist, so I work on children's books, comic books...nothing controversial.*

* But the government did investigate the comic book industry in the mid-1950s, leading to the *Comics Code.* Some companies shut down, and many writers and artists lost their jobs.

I'm active in the automobile workers union. Everyone in the union believes the Feds are on our tail. It's a scary time.

You've got to risk so much to engage in politics these days.

I know. I'd rather stay out of that...but I would *never* "name names" for the government and snitch on my friends.

Shortly before his death in 1950, the great English novelist and critic George Orwell meets the great French philosopher Michel Foucault. This imagined meeting occurs by accident in a Paris café. *

Foucault is in his early twenties, a recent university graduate who is beginning to embark on a brilliant writing career.

Orwell is in his late forties, a veteran man of letters and the author of nine books.

Chapter 10: POWER AND THE PEN

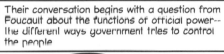

Their conversation begins with a question from Foucault about the functions of official power-- the different ways government tries to control the people.

What exactly is this thing you call "power"?

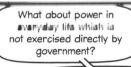

Consider the experience of World War II--of real, existing authoritarian and totalitarian governments in Germany and the Soviet Union-- and how they exerted control over their people. But also, in the so-called "democratic" nations. The problem of government control should be our chief concern.

What about power in everyday life which is not exercised directly by government?

The state sets certain rules and shapes how people interact and relate to one another. There are disciplinary mechanisms...

What exactly is this thing you call a "disciplinary mechanism?"

* This meeting between Orwell and Foucault never actually took place.

First, government may watch people with surveillance systems and *also* feed people to the lions. Government may watch to locate particular subjects--enemies--it wants to neutralize or sabotage.

George, there are broader aspects of control. There are the "undesirables" apart from state enemies--the mad, vagrants, prostitutes, blasphemers, orphans--which government sorts and segregates for the so-called "protection" of society.

In my work, I highlight control of the undesirables in national politics. Let's return to the surveillance question. My new book, *Nineteen Eighty-Four*, shows how a government imposes total surveillance on the people, even in the most private confines of the home.

The government, too, controls most forms of communication.

Can people find ways to counter official surveillance?

Maybe in small ways, but not effectively. The way my book unfolds, the political party rules with an iron fist. Their centralized powers to watch and punish are too great.

I have been thinking about where knowledge comes from. The idea how truth changes over the course of historical time.

Big Brother tries to control knowledge. Telling the truth becomes a revolutionary act.

Why did you title it *Nineteen Eighty-Four*? Is it science fiction?

It is a dystopian vision of a not-too-distant future.

The idea came to me near the end of World War II. I was reacting to the distortion of language I saw in official war propaganda.

In the novel, protagonist Winston Smith works in the Ministry of Truth, which deliberately promotes lies. Smith also rewrites historical documents and alters photographs for the ruling party.

In the nation of Oceania, the leader Big Brother is all-powerful, unquestionable, and sees everything.

Guardian of the Revolution...a mythic figure...No one has ever seen him in real life...He will never die.

BIG BROTHER

IS WATCHING YOU

BIG BROTHER

IS WATCHING YOU

BIG BROTHER

IS WATCHING YOU

BIG BROTHER

IS WATCHING YOU

His eyes seem to follow you about wherever you move.

The secret police enforce obedience to the state--speech, actions, and thoughts. The last is known as...

THOUGHTCRIME

Surveillance identifies the thought criminals--those who hold beliefs critical of the ruling party. Government tries to catch subversives who express any opposition. Police secretly mingle among the people, spreading false rumors.

Any dissenters they unearth are subjected to behavior-correcting torture in the notorious "Room 101."

It sounds like you have written a powerful and compelling novel. Surveillance can be used for very negative purposes. I hope your vision never becomes reality.

Few people know this, but my publisher asked J. Edgar Hoover for an endorsement of *Nineteen Eighty-Four*. He refused.

The government probably thought the book was a satire of America.

Orwell's *Nineteen Eighty-Four* became one of the best-selling books of the 20th century and remains popular today.

After the end of World War II, a new official surveillance infrastructure was established with the creation of the Central Intelligence Agency (CIA) in 1949 and the National Security Agency (NSA) in 1952. Both agencies focused on overseas intelligence gathering. The CIA emphasized human (or HUMINT) intelligence sources. It deployed spies and developed "friendly" contacts in foreign nations.

Chapter 11:
THE ABC'S OF SURVEILLANCE (CIA & NSA)

Meanwhile, the NSA focused on electronic and signals (SIGINT) interception. Its Echelon program, first developed in the 1960s, oversees the worldwide tracking of telephone, email, radio signals, satellite transmissions, and other electronic communications, with land-based spying centers in five nations--the U.S., England, Canada, New Zealand, and Australia.

During the Cold War, much of the focus was on the Soviet Union and its Communist allies. Today, the agencies engage the fight against terrorism and espionage by surveilling nations considered both friend and foe.

Despite its overseas focus, both the CIA and NSA have spied on Americans.

The CIA has no domestic law enforcement function. Yet, it has monitored Americans involved in political activity with a foreign policy connection, such as anti-war activity.

During the late 1960s and early 1970s, when social protest and unrest erupted across the nation, Presidents Lyndon Johnson and Richard Nixon used the Agency to track domestic protestors under a variety of programs--Project 2, Project Merrimac, Project Resistance, and Project Chaos.

Under Project Chaos, the Agency investigated "foreign influence" on the student anti-war movement. It issued special reports for the President with such titles as "Restless Youth" and "Student Dissent and Its Techniques in the U.S."

HELL NO - WE WON'T GO!

NO WAR!

POWER

The CIA built a network of informers who infiltrated dozens of groups and organizations. The Agency opened spy files on about 7,200 Americans. A special computer database held the names of about 300,000 civilians and referred to about 1,000 U.S. groups.

All of this surveillance revealed that foreign elements played no significant role within the peace movement. The CIA had cast unwarranted suspicion on thousands of people and undermined their civil liberties by spying on them.

Besides spying on Americans, the CIA conducted mind-control experiments on several thousand subjects. Under the now infamous Project MKUltra (1953-73), the CIA administered LSD and other drugs to study the reactions of subjects to harsh interrogation, including torture.

Other MKUltra experiments focused on isolation, sensory deprivation, and verbal and sexual abuse. They were conducted at universities, hospitals, and prisons.

Ted Kaczynski, "the Unabomber," was a test subject while an undergraduate at Harvard. He participated in a CIA-funded faculty research project where subjects underwent intensive verbal abuse.

Subjects were connected to electrodes that monitored their physiological reactions while facing bright lights and interrogated by an anonymous attorney. Subjects were individually belittled and humiliated based on their personal life histories. These tests were filmed and played back to the subjects to study expressions of impotent rage.

In all likelihood, this torturous experience impacted Kaczynski's development as a lone-wolf terrorist during the 1980s and 1990s. His political writings embrace anarchism and ecological justice. Before he was apprehended, Kaczynski mailed explosive devices to people on sixteen occasions, killing three and injuring twenty-three.

After Congressional investigations during the mid-1970s exposed CIA misconduct, the Agency claimed it left the domestic spy trade. In recent years, the scope of CIA spying on Americans largely remains unknown.

One public case occurred in 2014, when the Agency secretly hacked the work computers of U.S. Senators who were investigating overseas torture by the George W. Bush administration.

As the Senate Intelligence Committee prepared a major oversight report on U.S. torture, the CIA secretly snooped into their computers to get advance details on what the report was going to say.

Under Bush, the CIA ran several torture prisons and hid their existence from most policymakers. The torture at these prisons was worse than at other U.S. facilities at Guantanamo Bay in Cuba and Abu Ghraib in Iraq.

When confronted by Senate leaders, the CIA initially denied the spying charges. Later, the CIA director admitted the spying included reading the Senate Committee's emails.

Senator John McCain of Arizona was among the CIA's critics.

This is out of a movie... I really never believed that an agency of government, particularly with the capabilities of the CIA, would carry out such actions, which is clearly unconstitutional. In some ways, it's worse than criminal.

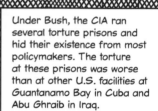

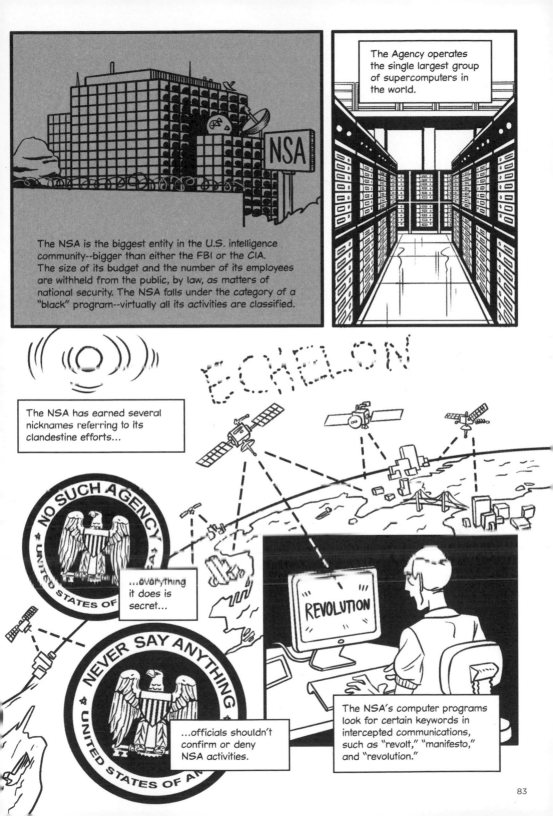

The NSA is the biggest entity in the U.S. intelligence community--bigger than either the FBI or the CIA. The size of its budget and the number of its employees are withheld from the public, by law, as matters of national security. The NSA falls under the category of a "black" program--virtually all its activities are classified.

The Agency operates the single largest group of supercomputers in the world.

ECHELON

The NSA has earned several nicknames referring to its clandestine efforts...

NO SUCH AGENCY · UNITED STATES OF A·

...everything it does is secret...

NEVER SAY ANYTHING · UNITED STATES OF AM·

...officials shouldn't confirm or deny NSA activities.

REVOLUTION

The NSA's computer programs look for certain keywords in intercepted communications, such as "revolt," "manifesto," and "revolution."

Soon after 9/11, President Bush secretly authorized the NSA to spy on Americans' communications.

The Agency began a new mission called the Terrorist Surveillance Program.

We have to "connect the dots."

Without getting a warrant, the NSA monitors the telephone calls and internet activity of millions of Americans. Everyone is a suspect without any specific evidence of wrongdoing.

The large telecom companies--AT&T, Verizon, and T-Mobile--collaborate with the NSA by turning over customer records. Under the PRISM program, the NSA also secretly obtains customer data from Microsoft, Apple, Google, and other companies.

Big Brother (government) and Little Brother (private companies) work together, forming a very dysfunctional family.

After the Terrorist Surveillance Program became public in 2005, Americans filed more than forty civil lawsuits against the telecom companies.

No litigant ever had their day in court. In 2008, Congress passed the FISA Amendments Act, which cleared the telecom companies of all liability for working with the government.

The lawsuits were dismissed. The secrecy of the Terrorist Surveillance Program remained intact.

Enter Edward Snowden, whose whistleblowing in 2013 shed new light on mass surveillance systems. The records obtained by Snowden revealed the NSA's motto:

"Collect It All."

There is the XKeyscore program for the internet. The programs Dishfire and Mobile Surge target cell phones. The program ICREACH has a "Google-like" search engine that sifts through more than 850 billion records.

The Agency is building a huge facial recognition database by gathering photo images from intercepted communications.

The new information about the NSA led to official deception.

James Clapper, director of U.S. National Intelligence, told Congress the NSA did not in any way spy on Americans. The statement was false.

Later, NSA director General Keith Alexander claimed during Congressional hearings that phone record data the Agency captured helped foil more than fifty terrorist plots around the world. Another lie.

In fact, the NSA's mass surveillance has proven ineffective in finding terrorists. As a federal judge found, the NSA stopped not one imminent attack or "otherwise aided the government in achieving any objective that was time-sensitive."

The U.S. government continues to view Snowden as a criminal. During his Presidency, Barack Obama rarely referred to Snowden.

I'm not going to dwell on Mr. Snowden's actions or motivations. I will say that our nation's defense depends in part on the fidelity of those entrusted with our nation's secrets. If any individual who objects to government policy can take it in their own hands to publicly disclose classified information, then we will never be able to keep our people safe, or conduct foreign policy.

Moreover, the sensational way in which these disclosures have come out has often shed more heat than light, while revealing methods to our adversaries that could impact our operations in ways that we may not fully understand for years to come.

This official defense of the NSA ultimately did not hold up. After a federal court found its spying to be unconstitutional, Congress made changes under the Freedom Act (2015).

However, the changes placed few new restraints on the scope of NSA surveillance activities...only on the storage and preservation of some records once they are collected.

While U.S. law and the Constitution guarantee the right to protest, the government has not been reluctant to monitor political challenges to the status quo. From the 1960s to the present, Americans who marched, signed petitions, subscribed to controversial publications, or joined activist groups might come under surveillance.

No blood for oil! Stop the war! Bring the troops home!

Jobs, Justice, Peace--Equal rights for all!

Organizing for change outside the two-party political system of the Democrats and Republicans is often viewed very negatively. Besides the FBI, city police and Military Intelligence of the U.S. Department of Defense entered the spy trade against protestors.

We demand justice now!

Dissent is patriotic!

Free speech is a right!

Chapter 12: SPYING ON SOCIAL PROTEST

Street protests are watched and sometimes filmed. Undercover agents may circulate in the crowd.

The people united will never be defeated!

Law enforcement and protestors hold very different attitudes about political activity and whether government surveillance in politics is justified.

We can't predict how these protests will change the nation.

These demonstrators are making trouble.

Without surveillance, we'd be left in the dark about their activities.

MEMBER LIST

SNCC

STUDENT

S.A.N

COMMITTEE FOR NUCLEAR

Real change never comes easily and is usually accompanied by marching in the streets. An important tradition of peaceful protest has helped to reform and improve society. However, law enforcement officials rarely greeted warmly such challenges to the status quo.

There is never enough political information to collect. One lead always suggests another.

How many cases are you working?

I can barely keep up with all the agitation. These people are so...radical!

During the last hundred years, the names of millions of Americans appear in secret spy files.

Civil rights and black power groups underwent state surveillance. The spy file on the Reverend Martin Luther King, Jr. was more than 17,000 pages.

We refuse to be treated like second-class citizens!

Returning violence for violence multiplies violence, adding deeper darkness to a night already devoid of stars.

King encountered heavy surveillance as he helped organize protests, including civil disobedience, against racial injustice.

Justice...by any means necessary... We declare our right to be respected as human beings.

The spy file on Malcolm X, leader of the Nation of Islam (NOI), totals about 11,000 pages. There are 333 pages of telephone wiretap transcripts from a single 1964 surveillance on his New York telephone.

On the night of his assassination in 1965, an undercover government operative secretly served as Malcolm X's bodyguard empowered to protect him. How can that be?

The FBI is the white man's devil.

Recently, law enforcement keeps a watchful eye on the Black Lives Matter movement by spying on their communications and infiltrating some of their demonstrations against police brutality.

Chapter 13:
THE "WAR ON TERROR"

America suffered a terrible tragedy on September 11, 2001. Almost three thousand people died at the World Trade Center in New York City, aboard Flight 93, and at the Pentagon.

Under President *George W. Bush*, the policies of the government began to be transformed to fight the new threat of terrorism.

The administration started a Global War on Terrorism (GWOT) against radical Islam--al Qaeda and its allies.

Three days after the attack, Bush visited Ground Zero. He addressed a gathering of first responders laboring to find the remains of the deceased and to clear the site.

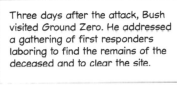

I can hear you. The rest of the world hears you. And the people who knocked down these buildings will hear all of us soon.

Whatever it takes. USA, USA, USA!

America today is on bended knee, in prayer for the people whose lives were lost here, for the workers who work here, for the families who mourn.

It had been many years since America was attacked by surprise on its home soil. Some people recalled the attack on Pearl Harbor in 1941, which prompted the U.S. entry into World War II.

The Homeland had been attacked. The American people felt profound pain and trauma and some wanted bloody revenge against the perpetrators.

Soon, the U.S. started wars in Afghanistan and Iraq to root out radical Islam.

Bush and the Congress sought to strengthen America's defenses. A new drumbeat for greater domestic surveillance spread throughout Washington. Echoing the Second Red Scare, officials promoted a high level of fear with dire new warnings about threats to many potential targets in America.

Congress passed the Homeland Security Act (2002) to restructure the Executive Branch. The Act created the new U.S. Department of Homeland Security (DHS), which took control over about two dozen federal agencies.

The new law goes into a lot of areas that have nothing to do with terrorism and a lot to do with the government and the FBI having a list of things they want to do.

Congress passed the USA Patriot Act (2001) without public hearings or debate. In the U.S. Senate, only Russell Feingold of Wisconsin voted against the Act.

The Patriot Act expanded the legal authority to monitor telephones and the internet.

The FBI also began to issue National Security Letters (NSLs) to obtain third-party records without legal warrants from banks, credit card companies, educational institutions, libraries, and medical providers.

Why is it necessary to collect so many records? Doesn't aggressive official surveillance pose a major threat to civil liberties?

Section 215 of the Patriot Act requires that people who turn over information to the government are forbidden to speak about it. Gag orders may be used to silence people.

Shh!

Hlph! Ah umph brvv!

The public is left in the dark about what the government is doing. Silence. No disclosure. Everything is a secret. Government keeps a lid on its deeds.

In 2002, the Pentagon started a huge computer datamining program called Total Information Awareness (TIA), a big database on Americans to make "connections between transactions."

Computers with artificial intelligence sort and match records.

They gather all available information from phones...

passports...

credit cards...

airline tickets...

driver's licenses...

rental cars...

gun purchases...

email...

web navigation...

and more.

After public outcry about the loss of privacy, Congress voted to defund the TIA program. This new surveillance initiative had scared the people. But Bush did not back away from mass monitoring.

Over the next several years, the Administration secretly put TIA into practice under other names and programs. As one example, the Investigative Data Warehouse (IDW) database run by the FBI now holds about two billion records on Americans.

The IDW uses "link analysis"--computer algorithms programmed to make connections by sorting through bulk data.

The election of Barack Obama in 2008 had little impact in pushing back the War on Terror's surveillance systems. In fact, Obama started new ones of his own.

Government remains busy building official watchlists--enticing or entrapping suspects to break the law, trying to eliminate encrypted electronic communications, and compelling online companies to report extremist speech to the government.

Surveillance also relied on unreliable forms of "behavioral detection." Police view people with suspicion based on their appearances.

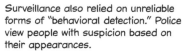

At airports, security agents study the body language of travelers to locate "suspicious" or nervous and fidgety passengers.

That man's face shows reddening. We should question him. He could be dangerous.

I have a *sunburn*! I was at the beach yesterday! I'm not a *terrorist*.

DHS began to promote a spying ethos for the public. The average person is told:

Be aware of the following suspicious behaviors. Individuals acting furtively and suspiciously. Individuals avoiding eye contact. Individuals departing quickly when seen or approached. Individuals in places they don't belong... an overloaded vehicle...over-dressed for the type of weather.

They want me to *stare* at people? It's rude. People get the wrong idea.

Today, the balance between the needs of national security and individual privacy is greatly weighted in the wrong direction. The War on Terror has led to a War on Privacy.

It is not enough to say "I have nothing to hide" and dismiss surveillance as harmless. This passive attitude merely serves to ratify dangerous practices.

As law professor Daniel J. Solove notes, "Privacy is rarely lost in one fell swoop. It is usually eroded over time, little bits dissolving almost imperceptibly until we finally begin to notice how much is gone."

Before 9/11, privacy rights in the U.S. were being advanced. Now, things have fallen apart and the lives of ordinary people face increasing scrutiny.

Former President Jimmy Carter, who helped reform FBI and CIA spying during the late 1970s, is another critic. He recently argued that U.S. conduct during the War on Terror...

...would have been unthinkable in previous times...While the country has made mistakes in the past, the widespread abuse of human rights over the last decade has been a dramatic change from the past.

The Occupy Wall Street (OWS) protest movement energized the nation when it burst onto the scene in the Fall of 2011.

It directly challenged the power of elite corporations and demanded change on behalf of the "99 percent."

Chapter 14: MONITORING THE 99%

The movement began on September 17, 2011, when activists set up a protest encampment in Zuccotti Park in New York City. Soon, encampments sprang up in other cities.

Protestors wanted to fight back against Wall Street, blamed for its role in creating an economic collapse a few years earlier. Their diverse set of demands centered around economic inequality: more equal distribution of income, bank reform, expanded job opportunities, student debt relief, and a reduction of corporate influence in politics.

The movement became popular, with over 1.5 million active followers on its social media pages. OWS published its own newspapers and sometimes set up live internet video feeds of the encampments.

While people under thirty dominated the encampments, supporters and allies came from many age groups and occupations.

President Obama publicly supported the *Occupy* movement, while also secretly directing government agents to track and crack down on it. In early October, Obama said: "I think it [*Occupy*] expresses the frustrations the American people feel." Later in the month, he said:

Some activists believed the police spied on them. They were correct. Besides more than 7,000 arrests, the intelligence community and local law enforcement surveilled *Occupy* groups in at least thirty-five cities.

"The most important thing we can do right now is those of us in leadership letting people know that we understand their struggles, and we are on their side."

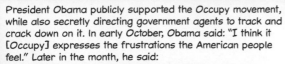

"OCCUPY BOSTON"

Their social media platforms and group meetings were put under surveillance. In some cases, police filmed the encampments.

Rather than respecting the First Amendment rights of protestors, DHS and FBI operated from a narrow social control perspective loosely linking the *Occupy* movement to "domestic terrorism."

No effort was made to analyze the variety of political perspectives within the movement...the many voices and disagreements. Little attention was paid to its democratic practices...how decisions were made through a community consensus process.

FIX CAPITALISM

END CAPITALISM

As one example of a major protest, Occupy Boston (OB) set up its first encampment at Dewey Square on September 30. Until mid-December, its street protests drew as many as a thousand people to the Square.

TOO BIG TO FAIL?

The lively encampment included a tent library, their own newspaper with a run of about 25,000 copies, and solidarity drum circles. They organized street demonstrations and served meals to hundreds of people a day.

College groups and labor unions aligned with Occupy actions.

At a rally at Harvard, protestors interrupted a speech by presidential candidate Newt Gingrich by using sarcastic mockery. They chanted,

Mic check / mic check / we love you Newt / thank you for standing up for corporations / they have rights too / thank you for understanding / that simple point / we are / the ninety-nine percent...

The Boston protestors were spied on. The official Boston Regional Intelligence Center (BRIC) collected and disseminated information on the movement in daily reports.

A BRIC analyst collected intelligence from Facebook and Twitter activity. They documented the mood of local protestors...public lectures related to the movement...the size and routes of upcoming protests...and plans for civil disobedience.

In mid-November, police began to break up encampments around the nation.

As a top Washington DHS official noted on November 14: "As 'Occupy' type protests continue to occur throughout the nation, several law enforcement organizations have undertaken steps to discontinue Occupy encampments within their jurisdictions or are in negotiations with demonstrators to close them down."

At least eighteen mayors participated in conference calls with police and intelligence officials seeking ways to end the Occupy movement.

After police evicted protestors in Zuccotti Park, the Boston Occupy General Assembly met to discuss a potential local crackdown. BRIC reported on "plans for if/when the camp is raided by Boston Police. OB called for emergency civil disobedience training and stated that college students and labor unions would be contacted to participate in protecting the camp."

The official intelligence sounded alarms about plans for resisting arrest.
BRIC circulated a special bulletin on the "possible concealment of razor blades and pins" by protestors in the event of arrest.

The razors could cut plastic hand restraints, while broken bobby pins might defeat handcuffs. The OB bulletin stated: "Officers are advised to exercise extreme caution when conducting pat downs and searches of any individuals involved in criminal activity."

A federal judge soon prohibited Boston police from shuttering the Occupy encampment. A court hearing would decide its fate. A few days before the ruling, BRIC detailed an Occupy meeting about an anti-eviction strategy.

☆ ☆ BRIC ☆ ☆

"OB voted to pass a proposal that would encourage people to go to the courthouse during the hearing. They specifically discussed holding signs outside the building and that it would be a bad idea to do this inside the courtroom. Additionally, this group will utilize Facebook, Twitter, and Blogspot to conduct a public relations campaign to gain support for OB."

At the court hearing, the judge put off a decision for two weeks, so the OB encampment remained alive. Finally, on December 7, the judged ruled against the encampment...police told protestors to leave Dewey Square at midnight the next day.

Anticipating a confrontation, BRIC reported that OB organized emergency non-violent civil disobedience training. OB also planned a special "dance party" when they were supposed to leave the Square. At the midnight deadline, a large crowd of more than a thousand people gathered at Dewey Square. Because of the size of the crowd, police announced they would not be making evictions.

However, eviction occurred the next day at 5 am when the crowd was much smaller. BRIC reported: "At the time of the raid there were about 80-100 people on site. Most protestors left the camp without incident; however, some protestors locked arms inside the camp and were subsequently arrested." In total, forty-seven individuals were taken into custody.

Despite the end of the encampment, Boston protestors continued to meet at alternative sites. BRIC continued with their reports for several more weeks. The last one was on January 5, 2012.

★★BRIC★★

"Please be advised that as of today the BRIC will no longer be disseminating a daily bulletin relative to Occupy Boston...BRIC will only disseminate products relative to Occupy Boston on an as-needed basis. Law enforcement and private sector security personnel are encouraged to review the main Occupy Boston website (www.occupyboston.org) for scheduling updates."

The spirit and politics of OWS lives on. When Senator Bernie Sanders of Vermont ran for President in 2016, he embraced much of the OWS agenda in his campaign.

Tonight, we served notice to the political and economic establishment of this country that the American people will not continue to accept a corrupt campaign finance system that is undermining American democracy, and we will not accept a rigged economy in which ordinary Americans work longer hours for lower wages, while almost all new income and wealth goes to the top 1%.

NOTE: This chapter is based on an article I wrote, "The State Response to Occupy," which is listed in the "Further Reading" page at the end of the book.

Chapter 15:

It is the view of the U.S. government that few communications should exist outside surveillance. As the NSA says, "Collect It All."

People who value their online privacy, and employ encryption to preserve it, may be viewed as dangerous suspects.

Somehow, preserving privacy is seen as guilty conduct. People who want privacy must be hiding something.

In the great Encryption Debate of the 21st century, the intelligence agencies are pressuring the large private telecom companies to eliminate encryption to help keep all records open for government inspection.

Encryption is good.
Encryption is for protection.
It empowers people.
Encryption is a privacy issue.
Who do you trust with your data?

THE ATTACK ON ENCRYPTION

Police agencies oppose encryption when it blocks their access to phone data. According to the FBI, the public's increased use of encryption means law enforcement is "Going Dark"...the bad guys are evading detection.

The Justice Department wants Congress to pass new laws to limit encryption. Tech companies should be forced to build special "back doors" into mobile phones to allow government to crack encryption.

This requires a new design to undermine existing phone security. Phones would be made wiretap-ready.

So far, Congress has not gone along with this police request.

The great Encryption Debate really is about the government wanting access to the personal information of everyone, not just criminals.

During the War on Terror, the use of encryption by alleged terrorists has not posed any real problem in preventing attacks. The official fear-mongering is being used to advance a "Collect It All" program.

Hands off my cell phone. I insist on protecting my data.

The FBI v. Apple fight was precipitated by a terrorist incident in San Bernardino, California. The phone of one of the two shooters--Syed Rizwan Farook--was recovered, but the Bureau couldn't access it because of Apple's strong encryption.

CRIME SCENE - DO NOT CROSS - CRIME S

CRIME SCENE - DO NOT CROSS - CRIME S

Although the shooter was already dead, the government insisted on getting all of the phone's data. When Apple opposed a court order, the encryption question was thrust into the national spotlight.

Most large tech companies-- Google, Facebook, Yahoo, Microsoft, and others--sided with Apple, as did most civil liberty groups. The issue is bigger than Apple... bigger than one company. It is about setting an industry standard about encryption and the privacy of digital communications.

The big internet service providers AT&T and Verizon sided with Apple... "strong encryption with no backdoors."

This is the most important moment in the battle over the future of technology, democracy, and free speech since the Edward Snowden revelations...

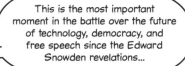

...said activist Evan Greer. While the encryption debate has been going on for 20 years, it now has reached a boiling point. How will it be resolved? Who are the winners and the losers?

Before a judge decided the FBI v. Apple dispute, the FBI backed down. It withdrew its demands on Apple to crack its own encryption.

Instead, the FBI managed to hire a private company to get into Farook's phone, but refused to say how it was done. Ultimately, no valuable information was found related to terrorism.

Then-FBI director James Comey admitted the issues represent...

...the hardest question I've seen in government, and it's going to require negotiation and conversation... It's really about who do we want to be as a country and how do we want to govern ourselves.

The encryption issue is likely to resurface before Congress. Stay tuned for the next chapter in the battle over encryption.

You know, I never realized that my phone had such good encryption.

I always assumed it got hacked by both cops and criminals.

Boy, we were wrong.

But for how much longer?

Live video surveillance in public spaces via Closed Circuit Television (CCTV) arrived in the U.S. in a big way within the last couple of years. CCTV cameras attached to utility poles, traffic lights, and the sides of buildings allow authorities to view urban street life at all times.

The new "security city" is an anonymity-free zone, a threatscape with no expectation of privacy for the public. Everyone is tracked.

Chapter 16: THE LIVE FEED

It happened first on a large-scale in London during the 1990s. Authorities say CCTV cameras help build a "Ring of Steel" in the city to prevent acts of terrorism and other forms of crime. Today, it is estimated that London dwellers are captured on CCTV at least 300 times per day.

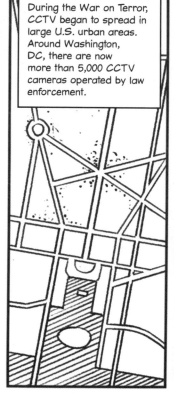

During the War on Terror, CCTV began to spread in large U.S. urban areas. Around Washington, DC, there are now more than 5,000 CCTV cameras operated by law enforcement.

In New York City, surveillance is most intense in the lower part of Manhattan--home to city government, Wall Street, and Ground Zero--which has more than 3,000 cameras. This area is officially labeled, like London, the "Ring of Steel."

The story of how a Ring of Steel was established in New York beginning in 2008 is illuminating. Leading political leaders eagerly supported CCTV. Mayor Michael Bloomberg and Police Chief Ray Kelly pushed for the plan.

There are collections of data, screening that we have to do to keep ourselves safe, that were unthinkable a few years ago...the argument against automation [of spying] is just this craziness that 'Oh, it's Big Brother.' Get used to it.

The local City Council expressed little resistance to spying. Councilman Peter Vallone, head of the Public Safety Committee, backed all new video monitoring programs.

Cameras are more important now than ever. They deter crimes just through the fact that they are there--anyone who says otherwise is completely wrong.

Part of the cost for the $90 million project was provided by the Department of Homeland Security. A former CIA official helped design the system, which was instituted without public input, outside oversight, or concern for privacy protections.

The Ring of Steel covers an area of only 1.7 square miles. There are cameras on every block.

Besides CCTV, about a hundred automatic license plate readers identify suspicious vehicles from information in a database...radiation detectors are planted in the street...moveable roadblocks control traffic...and extra police officers are on patrol.

The live video is watched by human cops and searched by computer programs looking for unattended packages and "suspicious" behavior. If a package is left unattended in the street for more than a prescribed time, a signal will alert police of its presence.

The computers can identify street images by shape, size, color, and movement. They can recognize a car circling in a "sensitive" location and will sound an alarm for security agents to check out.

The camera surveillance stretches into the nearby subway system and the memorial site at Ground Zero. There are about four hundred cameras at the memorial site--the most watched place in New York.

Despite the intensity of the surveillance, it may not prove effective in reducing crime, if the experience of London is any indication. For example, less than four percent of robberies caught on camera in London have been solved.

Making part of a city a police security zone reduces freedom in public. People may change their behavior if they know they are being watched. Who controls access to these videos?

CCTV exerts power. Some cameras can zoom in and out to locate subjects and track their moves.

Hey, you there!

CCTV spreads a surveillance culture of suspicion.

A few creative New Yorkers have mocked and satirized video surveillance by performing short plays in front of them. A small artist's group known as the Surveillance Camera Players has performed in front of the cameras since the mid-1990s. They developed more than a dozen different skits.

They also have led free walking tours through neighborhoods pointing out the public cameras in the area.

The Players wanted to create a spectacle to provoke public questioning about the role of surveillance in peoples' daily lives. They call their activity a "critical intervention" against pervasive surveillance and the loss of privacy.

The Surveillance Camera Players are part of a growing artistic movement challenging the new Surveillance Society, inspiring sister groups in Arizona, California, Italy, Lithuania, Sweden, and Turkey.

But the general public so far has not yet expressed much opposition to CCTV systems, which usually are established without popular debate or protest.

Chapter 17: The Harvesting of Social Media

Okay, social media surveillance...can you give me some examples?

The Department of Homeland Security ran a program called "Social Networking/Media Capability." It monitored dozens of popular websites, blogs, and message boards to locate popular opinion about news events that "reflect adversely" on the U.S. government.

So...they're looking for criticism of the government. What else?

Well, it's reported that surveillance included the following sites...

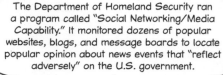

informed COMMENT
Thoughts on the Middle East, History and Religion

DRUDGE REPORT

CRYPTOME

myspace

flickr

hulu

WikiLeaks

JIHAD WATCH

WIRED

Government spy programs mine online media by matching and sorting their records as they endlessly trawl cyberspace. The harvesting of information is continuous and ever-present. The Machine never blinks, never sleeps.

The DHS spying program identifies more than 50 words or terms under the category of "domestic security" that, when identified in a communication, may be flagged for follow-up inspection.

The keywords include:

Looting

Attack

Lockdown

National preparedness

Homeland security

Authorities

Pipe bomb

Emergency landing

Militia

Cops

Toxic

Standoff

Dirty bomb

Threat

Domestic nuclear detection

Shots fired

But spying on the internet is a kind of wild-goose chase. Too much data now exists to make sense of it all. Those who spy are "drowning in data but starving for knowledge."

The vast and untamed internet will continue to be a social space where government struggles to keep up with what the people are saying and doing.

But online surveillance still means there is less free speech than many people recognize. Can we speak freely if political expression is under constant watch?

Epilogue: THE FLYING FUTURE

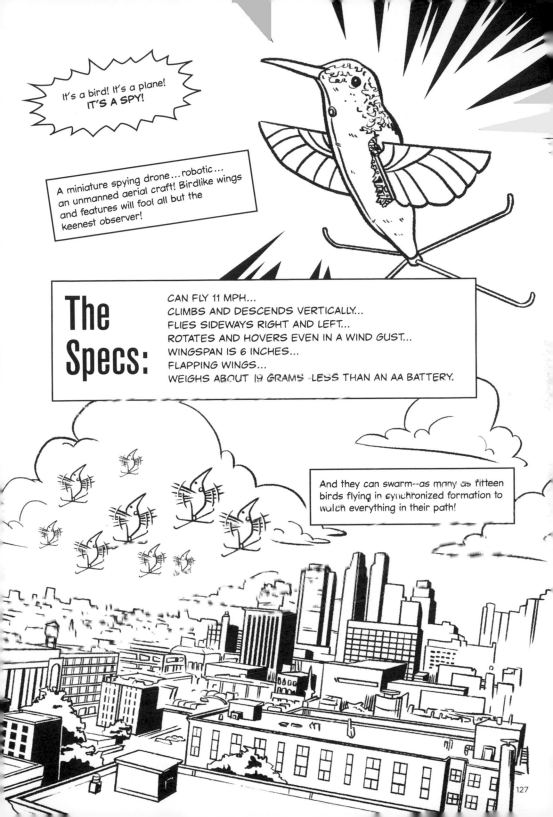

It's a bird! It's a plane! **IT'S A SPY!**

A miniature spying drone...robotic... an unmanned aerial craft! Birdlike wings and features will fool all but the keenest observer!

The Specs:

CAN FLY 11 MPH...
CLIMBS AND DESCENDS VERTICALLY...
FLIES SIDEWAYS RIGHT AND LEFT...
ROTATES AND HOVERS EVEN IN A WIND GUST...
WINGSPAN IS 6 INCHES...
FLAPPING WINGS...
WEIGHS ABOUT 19 GRAMS--LESS THAN AN AA BATTERY.

And they can swarm--as many as fifteen birds flying in synchronized formation to watch everything in their path!

127

Some Last Thoughts

Surveillance and spying have been around since ancient times, as readers of *The Machine Never Blinks* know well. But what is happening in the 21st century is unprecedented and dangerous — way beyond what even the feverish minds of conspiracy theorists and science fiction writers imagined in the past. Yesterday's Peeping Tom had only human eyes. Today, electronic eyes and ears can be so invasive they pose a real menace to the civil liberties of the people. We must not let the Peeping Toms win.

Protecting our privacy should be the natural order of things. It is an urgent matter. Your business is nobody's business but your own. No one should be spied upon without his or her consent. The new surveillance casts us all as suspects, as if we have something sinister to hide. It is starting to impact how we live. We are approaching the point where people have to prove their innocence, even though they have done nothing wrong.

If we don't do something about it soon, the new Surveillance Society may turn into a true nightmare. The capacity of the watchers to observe us and collect our data is rapidly advancing with the invention of all sorts of new technologies. It does not have to be this way. It is not inevitable. Limits need to be placed on the new technologies. People must demand that their leaders establish strict controls over the cameras, audio listening devices, geo-trackers, and internet monitoring and digital tools that leave us so exposed. We must say "no" in order to stop what is being taken from us.

A first step is to recognize the dimensions of the problem. In recent years, dozens of books have been published analyzing these issues. (See "Further Reading" on the following page for a short selection.) The depiction of surveillance in art, graphic novels, and comic books is just beginning to catch up. Everett and I have offered some important stories. There are many others still to be written. I believe graphic novels can lead the way to inform, and transform, the public's understanding of the perils of living in a surveilled world.

— *Ivan Greenberg*

Acknowledgements

This book grew out of discussions with artist Dean Haspiel, who drew covers for two of my books in the field of American history. We decided that a graphic project focusing on different topics surrounding surveillance could make a great new addition to the comics and graphic novel medium. Nothing like it had yet been published. Dean, whose work is always in demand, soon realized he was swamped with too many projects. Thank you, Dean, for all your help making this project a reality.

The task of drawing *The Machine Never Blinks* was given to Everett Patterson, whose style and knowledge made an excellent fit. I also want to thank Joan Hilty and Pete Friedrich of Pageturner Graphic Novels. They marshaled their skills to move the book along from start to finish. In the early stages, Joan's efforts included helping to edit the first part of the manuscript, bringing some order to an unruly draft. Pete's art consultation was invaluable.

A big thanks, too, to Fantagraphics Books and editor Mike Catron for staying the course.

— *Ivan Greenberg*

Further Reading

Angwin, Julia, *Dragnet Nation: A Quest for Privacy, Security, and Freedom in a World of Relentless Surveillance* (New York: St. Martin's Press, 2014).

Finan, Christopher M., *From the Palmer Raids to the Patriot Act: A History of the Fight for Free Speech in America* (Boston: Beacon Press, 2007).

Greenberg, Ivan, "The State Response to Occupy," in Todd A. Comer, ed., *What Comes After Occupy? The Regional Politics of Resistance* (Newcastle upon Tyne: Cambridge Scholars Publishing, 2015), 234-259.

Parenti, Christian, *The Steel Cage: Surveillance in America from Slavery to the War on Terror* (New York: Basic Books, 2003).

Priest, Dana, and Arkin, William, *Top Secret America: The Rise of the New American Surveillance State* (New York: Back Bay Books, 2011).

Solove, Daniel, *Nothing to Hide: The False Tradeoff Between Privacy and Security* (New Haven: Yale University Press, 2011).

Ivan Greenberg has been writing about surveillance for more than a decade and is a former college teacher. He is the author of *The Dangers of Dissent* (2010) and *Surveillance in America* (2012). He is finishing a new nonfiction book, *Suspicious Activity is Everywhere*. He lives in Washington, DC.

Everett Patterson is an illustrator and storyboard artist living in Portland, Oregon.

Joseph Canlas was born and raised in New Jersey and is a graduate of the School of Visual Arts.

Ralph Nader's unrelenting advocacy for the public over the years has led to safer cars, medicines, and workplaces, healthier foods, and cleaner air and water. *The Atlantic* named him one of the 100 most influential figures in American history. *Time* magazine called him the "U.S.'s toughest customer." He lives (and does battle) in the nation's capital.